Drum of Stone

HUMBERTO AK'ABAL

Drum of Stone

HUMBERTO AK'ABAL

Selected Poems

TRANSLATIONS BY

ROSEMARY BURNETT & JAMES ROBERTSON

KETTILLONIA

Published in 2010 by Kettillonia

Sidlaw House
24 South Street
Newtyle
Angus
PH12 8UQ

www.kettillonia.co.uk

ISBN: 978 1 902944 27 2

The publisher gratefully acknowledges the
financial assistance of the Scottish Arts
Council in the publication of this volume.

The publication of this book was timed to
coincide with Humberto Ak'abal's first ever
visit to Scotland. The publisher would like
to acknowledge the generosity of the Tom
Wright Trust in making this visit possible.

Printed by MPG Books Ltd, Bodmin

CONTENTS

Introduction *by Nigel Leask*   · 1
Introduction *by Humberto Ak'abal*   ·‖ 6

TUM AB'AJ

Chunan / Whitewaash / Whitewash   ⁞‖ 9
The granmither   ‖ 10
The thrawn yin   ·‖ 11
Flicht   ·‖ 11
The healer   ⁞‖ 12
Wantin tae greit   ⁞‖ 13
The wee auld wifie   ⁞‖ 13
Tum ab'aj   ⁞‖ 14
Grandfather   ‖‖ 15
Flowers of night   ‖‖ 15
The rattlesnake   ·‖‖ 16
Song   ⁞‖‖ 17

A WEE GLISK O THE SUN

Ri' kaqiq' / The air / The air   ⁞‖‖ 19
Wee oors   · 𝄞 20
A deid baukie   · 𝄞 20
A wee glisk o the sun   · · 21
Torol jab'   · · 21
The cranreuch   · ⁚ 22
Moonlit night   · ⁚ 22
The moon is mother   · ⁚ 23
Night name   · ⁚ 23
The hummingbird and the branch   · ⁚ 24
Messengers of the rain   · ⁚ 24
Song of light   · | 25
When it's breezy   · | 25
If a tree moves   · ·| 26
Earthquake   · ·| 26
Houses of adobe   · ⁚| 27
Ropop, ropop, ropop   · ⁚| 27
Xi'r-xi'r, lol-lol   · ⁚| 28
Serenade   · ⁚| 29

SOUTH AMERICA

IN MY LANGUAGE

Kinch'awik / I speak / I speak   · ·‖ 31

Tale   · :‖ 32

In the K'iche' language   · :‖ 33

Kasansananik   · :‖ 33

Ajxojolob'   · :‖ 34

Animal noises   · ‖‖ 35

Names of fungi   · ·‖‖ 36

Ri ja – The house   · :‖‖ 37

Tzel tzij – Ugly words   · :‖‖ 38

Je'l tzij – Beautiful words   · :‖‖ 39

In my language   : ⑥ 40

THE EMPTY DOORWAY

Chuq'ab / The effort / The trauchle   : : 43

A tellin   : ⦙ 44

Ma dreams   : ⦙ 44

It's late, I ken   : | 45

Thrawn hert   : | 45

The mute   : ·| 46

The last thread   : ·| 46

Toys   : :| 47

Lords of the night   : :| 47

I wanted to keep you   : :| 48

Wind of sorrow   : :| 48

Radiance   : ⦙| 49

Give me a thread   : ⦙| 49

The green shirt   : ‖ 50

Waiting for your return   : ‖ 50

Tears in sleep   : ·‖ 51

Trapped heart   : ·‖ 51

The round puddle   : :‖ 52

Mist in the afternoon   : ⦙‖ 53

THE MORN'S MORN

Xaqje'are / Himself / Himsel : ||| 55

The deid-kist : ·||| 56

Freedom : :||| 57

Prayer : :||| 57

Nicanor : :||| 58

The morn's morn, mibbe : :|||| 58

Auld claes : :|||| 59

Yin o thae : ⑥ 60

That efternune : · 61

Pak'lom mountain : : 62

Yellow flower of the graveyards : : 63

A note on the K'iche' language and pronunciation : ·|| 71

A note on the Maya numeric system : :|| 72

Introduction

by Nigel Leask

HUMBERTO AK'ABAL hails from Momostenango, near Totonicapan, in the pine-forested K'iche' Highlands of Guatemala. The town is famous for its chamarras or woollen blankets, and a notable centre of Mayan language and culture. After working as a blanket weaver and shepherd, Ak'abal migrated to Guatemala City where he found employment as a street vendor and market porter. Success as a poet has enabled him to return to his village and devote himself exclusively to his art. He writes both in his native Mayak'iche' language and in Spanish, and is fascinated by the question of bilinguality, which makes the present translation into both English and Scots especially appropriate.

Deftly rendered by Rosemary Burnett and James Robertson, these translations capture the dual linguistic world of Ak'abal's poetry, his ability to switch easily between Spanish and Mayak'iche', the latter rooted in the spoken language of his village. Although the haunting, aphoristic quality of many of his lyrics comes straight from the heart of Ak'abal's own Mayan world, translation into Scots adds a very special dimension to their passage across cultures. It is facilitated by the colloquial immediacy of Robertson's Scots, but the translation also makes skilful use of the Scots literary tradition. For example, 'A wee glisk o the sun' develops the concentrated diction of MacDiarmid's 'The Watergaw', with its evocation of the ephiphany, the 'antrin thing' central to both MacDiarmid's and Ak'abal's lyrics. In fact there's an uncanny resemblance between MacDiarmid's early verse in *Sangschaw* and *Penny Wheep* and Ak'abal's poetry, which makes this translation especially appropriate.

Despite the political predicament of the Mayak'iche' people discussed below, Ak'abal denies harbouring any post-colonial grudge against the language of his people's oppressors, and is happy to write in Spanish, not least for the purposes of reaching an international audience. As he puts it, 'the Spanish that I use to communicate with a wider public is based in the cosmogony of my own cultural roots... bilingualism has permitted me to see my environment from a different perspective... writing in Spanish doesn't make me any less K'iche', or any better as a writer'.[1] Like the gourd song in 'The Healer', poetry in either language has a curative power, especially in a society like modern Guatemala, distempered by racial and linguistic conflict.

'We resist from the depth of our culture', writes Ak'abal in 'Yellow Flower of the Graveyards', the final poem in the present volume. It's a dark poem, and the only one here that explicitly addresses the political plight of his people since the brutal conquest of the advanced Mayak'iche' civilisation by Pedro de Alvarado in 1524. (Today Maya-speaking indigenous groups make up 65% of Guatemala's population of 13 million). But the placement of 'Yellow Flower' at the end of this volume is judicious, because Ak'abal's characteristic mode is one of lyrical intensity rather than direct political protest. That's apparent to the reader of the present selection, as he or she works through a body of poems concerned with voice and language, memory and forgetting, life and death, birds, beasts and trees, moonlight and darkness, lost love, and hopes for the future ('the morn's morn'), before arriving in the wasteland of contemporary Guatemalan politics.

It's important however to grasp the wider context of Ak'abal's poetry. Unlike their more fortunate neighbours in Mexico, Guatemalans never experienced a revolutionary overthrow of the neo-colonial state; consequently the authoritarian rule of a tiny empowered minority of feudal caudillos, fruit-company capitalists and military dictators has persisted to our own times. The overthrow of the reformist Arbenz/Arevalo administrations by a US-backed military coup in 1954 led to over three decades of bloody civil war between government forces and Marxist guerrilla movements, after 1982 united under the aegis of the 'URNG', or Guatemalan National Revolutionary Union.

This movement was supported by over half a million people, mainly Maya-speaking campesinos from the western and central highlands and the region known as El Peten. As well as a class struggle, the civil war took the form of an ethnic conflict between government-supported Ladinos (Spanish-speaking Guatemalans of largely mestizo background) and the indigenous Maya majority. In 1982 one wealthy landowner notoriously excused the bloodshed on the grounds that 'the massacre of Indians is simply the continuation of the

---

1   Humberto Ak'abal, *Las Palabras Crecen* (Seville: Sibilina, 2009), p.5

conquest'. The government's war against Guatemala's indigenous population peaked in the 1980s under the presidency of General Efraín Rios Montt, in a genocidal crusade known as la escoba (the broom), which saw the systematic destruction of hundreds of villages, and the torture and massacre of their inhabitants. In 1996 a peace accord was finally signed, bringing to an end the 36-year civil war in which it is estimated that over 200,000 Guatemalans died and a million were made homeless. Unlike contemporary struggles in El Salvador and Nicaragua, this appalling bloodbath passed relatively unnoticed in Europe and the USA.

'Justice doesn't speak our language' writes Ak'abal in 'Yellow Flower'. The end of the civil war has sadly offered few signs of amelioration for the Maya people: Guatemala has seen nothing like post-apartheid South Africa's Truth and Reconciliation process. The award of the Nobel Peace Prize to the indigenous Mayak'iche' activist Rigoberta Menchu in 1992 certainly focused international attention upon its unhappy plight. Nevertheless, not only have the butchers of the government's PACs ('Civil Defence Patrols') never been brought to account, but many have recently been awarded compensation payments by the authorities. Little wonder that Ak'abal paints a Blakean picture of birds 'keechin' on 'kirks and courthooses' 'wi aw the freedom o yin that kens/ that god and justice /belang the sowl' and not the judiciary. When Bishop Juan Gerardi, coordinator of the Guatemalan Human Rights office, was murdered outside his home in 1998 two days after blaming the army for the 200,000 civil war deaths, it was apparent that truth was the main casualty of the ongoing repression. The perpetrators, including Efraín Rios Montt, not only enjoy impunity, but continue to run the country, at least behind the scenes. In 2002, the UN human development index ranked Guatemala as 120th of the world's 173 countries, lowest of any country in the Western hemisphere other than Haiti. This is the dark background to Ak'abal's poetry, a society in which 60% of Guatemala's Maya people continue to be the victims of racial discrimination and oppression, despite the fact that 'the Maya trail' has become a popular Western tourist attraction: 'landowners exploit us/ religions confuse us, / And the tourist offices exhibit us'.

The poems in this collection will speak for themselves, and the translators have wisely opted to include a number of poems in the original K'iche', which

Ak'abal describes as 'a poetic, guttural language, rich in onomatopoeas'. (Try reciting 'Axojolob', or 'Animals Voices', as sound poetry, after consulting the 'notes on pronunciation'). The world view and cultural predicament of the Mayak'iche', and the rich resources of an ancient but proscribed language, are astutely communicated by these translations. The very act of utterance is itself a political act: 'I speak so as to gag the mouth of silence' ('tae steek/ the mooth/ o silence' in Robertson's Scots rendition). Ak'abal underlines the oral and popular inspiration of his verse, but we shouldn't forget that Mayak'iche' is also the language of one of the world's greatest written texts, the 16th century Maya cosmogony or 'Book of Council' known as the Popol Vuh.

Like Ak'abal's poetry, the Popol Vuh was itself written as an act of resistance, under the proscription of a foreign language and religion. Composed in the Latin alphabet in the aftermath of Spanish conquest, the book's anonymous Maya authors speak of basing their narrative on a lost original, written in the complex hieroglyphics of the Classical Maya civilization. 'There is the original book and ancient writing, but the one who reads and assesses it has a hidden identity'. The Popul Vuh was only published in translation from manuscript in 1857; it has recently been made available to English readers by Dennis Tedlock, working in collaboration with the Mayak'iche' spiritual leader Andres Xiloj Peruch from Momostenango, the hometown of Humberto Ak'abal.[2] It's a magnificent compendium of narratives and rituals that continued to be transmitted in Mayak'iche' down to the present, suturing the traumatic wounds of the conquest and the repression that followed. But like 'Tum ab'aj', the 'drum of stone' (the poem which lends its title to this volume), the book is a secret: 'Those who don't know it/ would pass by without seeing'.

Aka'bal has recently written that 'my poetry is marked by the feel, the sight, and the understanding of my maternal language (Mayak'iche'); it follows that I interpret the world, my world, according to the cosmogony of my ancestors'.[3]Perhaps the Popul Vuh, with its narrative of successive creations, and the constant interchange between the divine, human and animal worlds, offers a key to the potent natural symbolism of Ak'abal's verse. It's a world in which every stone, tree, animal, bird has a hidden meaning, in which the stars

---

2   *Popol Vuh: The Definitive Edition of the Mayan Book of the Dawn of Life and the Glories of Gods and Kings*, translated by Dennis Tedlock (revised edition, New York and London: Simon & Shuster, 1996).

3   *Las Palabras*, p.5

are mirrored in the frost ('The Cranreuch'), or 'the rain's drizzle is the hair of a beautiful woman' ('Grandfather'), with its mythic and sacred overtones. Yet just as Ak'abal is willing to write in Spanish as well as Mayak'iche', he also acknowledges the importance of his readings in 'universal literature'; this is a modern, transcultural poetry of confluence, albeit one steeped in deep cultural traditions. Ak'abal's poetic utterance refuses the dumbness of the 'wee auld wife', brought on by 'steekin her gab in her pain'. As he confesses in 'In my Language', 'I don't know what it is for, but even so, I persist', indicating the fragility of these lyrics. Sometimes, he writes, 'the effort of forgetting is also poetry', although the dominant impulse here is to weave the silent cultural memory of his people into a poetic fabric that will refuse oblivion. The best that can be hoped for, in the present, is that in 'the morn's morn, mibbe, this will aw chynge'. The poems translated here bear witness to that hope.

NIGEL LEASK
Regius Professor of English Language and Literature,
University of Glasgow

Introduction

THE FIRE BURNED AND OCCASIONALLY BOOMED... 'The pictures in the flames are not just there by coincidence, the fire is a voice, the fire is a messenger.'

The pots and cooking stones were blackened, the walls too. Night didn't enter the kitchen because it was darker inside than out.

'It's going to rain, it feels cold and the wind is thickening...'

My mother understood the song of the birds, the voices of the animals and the language of physical phenomena.

'Don't go out into the patio because the storms are going to start, the dog isn't biting his tail for the love of it, the thatch isn't writhing of its own volition...'

It began to rain. The thunderclaps and the lightning flashes gave the impression that the sky was about to fall in. The lightning that entered the kitchen seemed like the boastings of silvery water. The echo of the storm drowned itself between the gullies and the night disappeared beneath the cloudburst. On nights like these, mother told us a story.

'The tree at the back of the house is witness to what I am going to tell you...'

We began to feel a little afraid.

'That pot there (and she pointed to an earthenware pot behind me), in the olden days it would take human form, eyes would sprout, and ears, and it would poke its tongue out...'

Slowly, I moved to one side, still listening to her every word, but moving away from the pot.

'Don't be frightened, it doesn't do that any more.'

'Why didn't you break it so that it wouldn't frighten you any more?'

'Because this pot was made by the Spirits of our ancestors, and if we break it today, it would be whole again tomorrow…'

The old pot, sitting in a corner of the kitchen, seemed like a deaf, dumb and blind head. Slowly, the fire died, and mother scattered the embers.

'Look at this little flame: it's the flower of the fire. They say that if your day has come gold will appear between the embers, and that is why, when the fire dies down, you must always rake through the ashes – if there's nothing today, then maybe tomorrow…'

Only a thread of smoke remained in the fireplace.

The years have passed, my mother is tired, the house has changed. When I ask her to tell me a story again, she sighs and smiles…

'Times have changed, it doesn't make sense any more to tell those stories under an electric light. In those days, it gave me joy because the light of the kindling gave a special light. But now even the ghosts have fled and every day I am more and more tired and my memory isn't what it was… Now it's your turn to make up your own stories and tell them to your children.'

She looked and me and her quiet serene expression was of one who knows that she has done her duty of having passed the responsibility on to others…

My mother passed on to me her restlessness and her love of words. My stories and poems are an attempt to continue the tradition of my elders, and are also a way of prolonging my mother's voice with my own words.

HUMBERTO AK'ABAL

TUM AB'AJ

Chunan

Iwir, ximuq ri kaminaq.
Kamiq, kachunax ri ja.

We katzalijik uloq
man kuriq ta chi ri', ri ub'e.

Ri usaqil ri chun,
chi uwech ri usaqil ri ik',
kumoyij ri kib'oq'och ri kaminaqib'.

Whitewaash

Yestreen, the yirdin o the deid.
The-day, the whitewaashin o the hoose.

Gin he wins hame
He'll no ken the wey ony mair.

The white o the limewaash
in the licht o the mune
blins the een o the deid.

Whitewash

Yesterday, the burial,
Today, the whitewashing of the house.

If he returns
He will no longer find his way.

The whiteness of the limewash,
in the light of the moon,
blinds the eyes of the dead.

The granmither

The nicht begins
wi the mune
– granmither o the touns –
comin oot wi her cauk-white caunle
tae licht up the lown.

The daurkness
derns in the cleuchs,
the wee birds
rowe up their sangs
and the trees
lean on their ain shaddas.

The granmither
that for centuries hasna fawn ower
faws
intae the een o the nicht.

The thrawn yin

The thrawn wee laddie,
ayewis lookin ahint,
fankled himsel in some ruits
and fell doun.

Stertit tae skreich.

Felt his granny's vyce
like a chap on the heid.

'When a dug's daein a shite
in the middle o the road,
dinna you stare
or ye'll get whit's comin tae ye.'

Flicht

He hid himsel
ahint the stane
that wis in the courtyaird.

He shithered wi fear
because they were huntin him
sae they could pou the heid aff him.

The granmither tellt
hoo the stane raxed
and happit Juan.

He jouked awa
and the day efter
the stane wis awa anaw.

The healer

Ma granfaither wis no weel.

Speelin bens
and crossin glens
we gaed lookin for the healer.

Maister Tun
wis a sonsie auld man.

He took a toom gourd
and sang intil it.

'Tak it tae him that he mey drink the sang.'

Ma granfaither pit the gourd
up tae his lugs
and bit by bit his face chynged,
and the nixt day he begun tae sing
and syne even tae dance.

Wantin tae greit

The clachan yince wis fou
o ghaists.

Noo ye dinna see them
onywhaur at aw
and naebody speaks o them nae mair.

There's times
I feel like greitin
because I kent them:
they learnt me fear.

The wee auld wifie

Thon wee auld wifie
grat aw day and aw nicht.

Naebody kent the cause o her dool,
naebody kent whit for she wis greitin.

Some said it wis the cauld,
ithers said she wis hurtit.

The wee auld wife became dumb
wi steekin her gab on her pain.

She bydit alane and wis aw swallied up
in the flames o her wae.

Tum ab'aj

In my village there is a big stone
which we call Tum ab'aj.

The sun and the moon care for it.

It is not a silent stone,
it is a drum of stone.

It's covered with a downy cape
which we call toad's crap.

A path, a river,
and the stone in the middle.

Those who don't know it
would pass by without seeing.

The old ones, no;
they stop,
they burn incense and resin,
candles and honey.

When it rains, the stone sounds;
tum, tum, tum, tum...

Grandfather

My grandfather said
that the rain's drizzle
is the hair of a beautiful woman
who runs past
between the trees.

If a bachelor sees her
he knows that behind her
comes the happiness of his heart.

Flowers of night

When there was no moon
I went out to sit
behind the house.

One time
my mother followed me
and asked me what I was doing.

I told her that I loved to see
how the flowers of the night
lit up and went out.

The rattlesnake

The old man of the village
brought a gourd
and a rattle.

He started to dance
round the rattlesnake
and said to it:
'Come into the gourd
and I will take you to your mountain,
come into the gourd
and I will take you to your mountain…'

At the mouth of the gourd
the old man shook his rattle.

And the snake
went into the gourd
and went back to his mountain.

Song

The grandfather, by the hand,

led his grandson

to greet the trees,

to chat to them,

to caress their bark,

to smell their leaves…

and the trees

sang their names.

A WEE GLISK O THE SUN

Ri kaqiq'

Kaxojow ri kaqiq,
kulik'ik'ej ri uxik' xuquje' katsutinik.

Ri kaqiq' are jun nimalaj chikop,
ri karapap chi kaj
naj puqi'ri kaj.
Rumal ri',
xa kaquna' ri utewal ri uxik'.

The air

The air dances,
spreads its wings and turns circles.

The air is a large bird,
which flies high
high up in the sky;
And so
we only feel the draught of his wings.

The air

The air dances,
spreids its wings and birls aboot.

The air is a muckle bird,
fleein heich
heich awa in the lift;
and sae
aw we feel is the souch o his wings.

Wee oors

In the heich oors o the nicht
stars strip aff
and douk in the rivers.

Hoolets grein for them,
the wee feathers on their heids
birse up.

A deid baukie

And there it's there, ahint the hoose,
forleitit, a deid baukie-bird
faan doun frae the bauks…

Hoo mony rains
fullt this bleck umberellae
tae at last it had nae wings?

A wee glisk o the sun

This efternune
efter thunner and storms
the lift gied us
a wee glisk o the sun.

The birds chant
and the trees greit
wi the new-faan rain.

Torol jab'

He gaed gyte amang the brainches
o the gean tree,
frae his thrapple
he unsteekit a sang
and his flauchterin wis a fiesta.

In this wey the cushie doo
opened its doors
tae the rain.

The cranreuch

In the cranreuch
the stars drew portraits o themsels.
Wi the dawn
cam a dug lickin the gress,
or, wha kens,
mibbe he wis eatin stars.

Moonlit night

That moonlit night
the coyote appeared
on the barren hillside.

It seemed as though he came
out of the sky
or as if the hillside
was giving birth.

He arrived at the river's edge
and drank water.
and he howled
auuuuuu… auuuuuu…

The moon is mother

The moon is the mother
of the colours
which don't know the day.

She displays them
in reverse.

Night name

Tukur, tukur, tukur…
Owl, owl, owl…
The owl sings
his night name.

Turu', turu', turu'…
Let him go, let him go, let him go…
The bird speaks
of someone who is ill.

Muq'u, muq'u, muq'u…
Death, death, death…

The hummingbird
and the branch

The hummingbird and the branch
tangled together
in the tresses of the sun
after the cloudburst.

Messengers of the rain

The song of the mockingbirds
heralds the arrival
of the rain.

The fireflies
with their dance of yellow lights
tell us that the rain is near.

And when the toads
take off their stone clothes
dark clouds blot out the sky
and the first drops of rain
start to fall.

Song of light

When the sun
starts to sing its song of light
the woodpecker
comes out to look
through the window of his house
and he smiles.

When it's breezy

When the wind blows
strongly
trees embrace trees.

Their branches intertwine
and they make love.

A little time later
the trees set flowers
and give birth to fruit.

If a tree moves

If a tree moves
from one side to the other
it's because the fruit
is tickling it.

And its flowers fall.
They've laughed their heads off.

Earthquake

The trees
hold fiercely
to the ground
and when it quakes
their branches hang from the sky.

Houses of adobe

After the rains
I walked through the village
and in each puddle
I saw the reflections of
the adobe houses.

After the rains
the earthen streets
were little rivers of mud
and the village smelt new.

Ropop, ropop, ropop

Ropop, ropop, ropop, ropop…
The vultures shake out their wings
and from the branches of a cypress tree
they watch over their food.

Utz, utz, utz, utz…
'It's maturing nicely,'
they say amongst themselves.

The vultures come down from the tree
and they eat the dead dog,
they even close their eyes
to savour it.

Xi'r-xi'r, lol-lol

Xi'r, xi'r, xi'r, xi'r …
The song of winter
from beneath the leaves.

Xi'r, xi'r, xi'r, xi'r …
The crickets announce
the arrival of the rains.

Lol, lol, lol, lol …
the song of summer
on the fallen leaves.

Lol, lol, lol, lol …
The rains go away
with the cicadas' farewell.

Serenade

B'ir, b'ir, b'ir, b'ir…
B'ir, b'ir, b'ir, b'ir…

B'iri, b'iri, b'iri, b'iri…
B'iri, b'iri, b'iri, b'iri…

Krik-krik-krik-krik…
Krik-krik-krik-krik…

The solemn notes
are those of the old ones.

The soft notes
are those of the females.

The sharp notes
are those of the young crickets.

Bi'r, b'ir, b'ir, b'ir…
Bi'ri, b'iri, b'iri, bi'ri…
Krik-krik-krik-krik…

IN MY LANGUAGE

Kinch'awik

Kinch'awik
che utz'apix
ri uchi'
ri tz'inowik.

I speak

I speak
so as to gag
the mouth
of silence.

I speak

I speak
tae steek
the mooth
o silence.

Tale

The tale is tellt
o an auld, auld people.

Scunnered wi their ain tung – sae it's said –
they set themsels tae biggin a ben –
mool upon mool –
till it raxed up intae the cloods.

Up yonder, it wis tellt,
they haundit oot languages.

Sae they thocht they'd try it oot…

Ye had tae hae baws tae get up there.
The first thing tae dae
wis cowp a wheen muckle drams.

On the wey back doun,
ye were jist haiverin, pure pish…

but in anither language!

In the K'iche' language

In K'iche'
we don't say goodbye

We say *kantich' ab'ej chik*
(I'll talk to you again)

Kasansananik

Kasansananik,
Kasansananik, nana
kasansananik.

Ri q'ojom
kasansananik
kamiq'ow ri nimaq'ij.

Kasansananik
kasansananik.

Kasansan ri q'ojom
kaxojlin ri tzu.

Kasansananik,
kasansananik, tata
kasansananik.

Ajxojolob'

(the dancers)

For Nakil

Tzin Tzilintzín, tzin tzilintzín
tzoj, tzojtzoj, tzoj tzojtzoj.

Tzilintzín, tzojtzoj,
tzilintzín, tzojtzoj.

Pungún, plenguén
pungún, plenguén.

Tzin tzilintzín, Tzin tzilintzín,
tzoj tzojtzoj, tzoj tzojtzoj.

Tzilintzín, pungún,
Tzilintzín, pungún.

Tzojtzoj, plenguén,
Tzojtzoj, plenguén.

Tzilintzín, tzojtzoj,
Tzilintzín, tzojtzoj,
Tzilintzín, tzojtzoj…

Animal voices

Ajaw, ajaw, ajaw…
Naw, naw, naw…

Saqiriq'ij, saqariq'ij, saqariq'ij…
Xt'oj-t'oq-toqiiik, xt'oq-t'oq-t'oqiiik…

Ch'iw, ch'iw, ch'iw…
Q'ol, q'ol, q'ol…

Cholchik, cholchik, cholchik,
Q'or, q'or, q'or…

Kus, kus, kus…
Wuuu, wuuu, wuuu…

Utiwww, utiwww, utiwww…
Q'ur, q'ur, q'ur…

B'eee, b'eee, b'eee…
Choq'ij, choq'ij, choq'ij…

Names of fungi

Uxikin kowilajche'
(Ears of evergreen oak)

Uraq' mazat
(Deer's tongue)

Uraqan xar
(Bluebird's foot)

Upan ib'oy
(Armadillo's belly)

Uraqan tuktuk
(Woodpecker's feet)

Ri ja – The house

Uchi' ja
(Mouth of the house),
door.

Ub'oq'och ja
(eyes of the house),
windows.

Uwi' ja
(hair of the house),
roof.

Raqan ja
(feet of the house),
hallway.

Utza'n ja
(nose of the house),
corners.

Upam ja
(stomach of the house),
inside.

Ja,
house.

Tzel tzij – Ugly words

Palaj nuwachaq
My arse's face.

Maj unan
You have no mother.

Ujolom xk'ub'
Cooking-stone head.

Paxinaq upalaj
Split-face.

Chaqij achaq
Dried shit.

Utiw maj uware
Toothless coyote.

Pachal rij
Hunchback.

Uraqan ch'ok
Blackbird feet.

Yutu't uxikin
Shrunken ears.

Sal urij
Rash-face.

Tze' maj uware
Toothless smile.

Nin
Stinker.

Je'l tzij – Beautiful words

Uxere tura's
Cheeks like peaches.

Ub'oq'och ch'umil
Eyes like stars.

Cho ukayib'al
Intense gaze.

Ujoronal k'ux
Freshness of the soul.

Ajk'amal b'e
Guide of the paths.

Kotz'i'j uk'ux
Flowering heart.

Ujolom tinimit
Head of the village.

Q'axal q'aq'
Bringer of fire.

Uk'ux b'urb'ux ja'
Heart of the spring.

Ki'utzij
Soft wordsmith.

Uruxlab' ja
Perfume of the house.

Ajkunanel b'is
Healer of sadness.

In my language

In my language
poetry is called:

Aqajtzij
(honey words).

Je'ltzij
(beautiful words).

Pach'umtzij
(embroidered words).

All in all
I don't know what it's for,
but even so,
        I persist.

THE EMPTY DOORWAY

Chuq'ab

Ri chuq'ab ri kaqokoj che ri
usachik sataq xuquje xik'ali.

The effort

The effort of forgetting
is also poetry.

The trauchle

The trauchle o mismindin
is poetry tae.

A tellin

The mune wis a muckle hoose
sittin on the rigbane o the ben.

Gin ma faither gied me a tellin
I'd awa tae the mune
and kip there.

Ma dreams

Ma dreams in shivereens
like hail-puckles
are skailt amang the stanes:
ae kiss o the sun turns them tae mist,
ae fuff o wund
turns them tae nocht.

It's late, I ken

In yer hert
There's nae room ony mair.

It's late.

I jist want ye tae ken
that forenent yer door
a gaberlunzie man is
waitin.

Thrawn hert

That efternune
ma hert turnt itsel ower
and landit on its heid.

When I kent
that ye didna luve me
it stertit tae whummle.

It's you that's tae blame
noo that ma hert is thrawn for aye.

The mute

She steyed hyne awa.
Sundays she cam doun tae the toun
tae sell peaches.

I waited on her by the auld brig.
She gied me a bonnie look,
and mibbe she wis hopin for a word back frae me.

I looked at her and ma mooth turnt tae watter
and I couldna say onythin.

The nixt day, somebody spiered her aboot me
and she said
she didna want a man
that wis a mute.

The last thread

The last thread
of the light of day
bends
under the weight of the night
and does not break.

It's like hope.

Toys

I looked at the toys
of the other kids
and, just looking,
the day passed me by.

One night I dreamt
that I had one.

Since then
I have not wanted
to wake.

Lords of the night

Dreams
watch over the paths
of the night.

They go on ahead to see
what is round the corner.

Then they return
to tell you
and you think you're dreaming.

I wanted to keep you

I wanted to keep you
as the birds keep their song
in their hearts.

But, you see,
without knowing how,

your name
has fallen
from my hands.

Wind of sorrow

This wind of sorrow
which blew in your eyes
snuffed out your burning gaze.

Who wounded your joy?

Who?

Radiance

I pursued you
in the market
like the river
runs after foam.

'I'm not the only woman
you wag your tail at,'
you told me.

'There is only one moon in the sky,'
I answered you.

'There are also stars,'
you replied.

'Yes, but those which are near the moon
cannot be seen
because her radiance
makes them disappear.'

Give me a thread

Give me a thread, spider,
I want to weave a song
for her.

Or, if you like,
weave her a poem
and I will find you the words.

The green shirt

I put on
that green shirt,
it was rather old.

And my best trousers,
the trousers had some patches
but they were clean.

I stopped
underneath that cypress
where the grey owls
have their nest.

You appeared
on the curve of the road
and you passed in front of me
as though I were
just another owl.

Waiting for your return

Whenever this door is closed
its rusted hinges complain
as though they wanted to remain open,
awaiting your return.

This empty doorway refuses to believe
that you will never come back.

Tears in my sleep

Sometimes I feel
a great sadness,
so great
it's as big as the wind.

I cry until my eyes run dry.

And I wake
with the strange feeling
of one who has wept
beside a corpse
and seen a dream turn to ashes.

Trapped heart

There are nights when
the light of the moon falls violently
and the heart stays trapped,
unable to flee into the darkness
where forgetfulness lives...

The round puddle

The round puddle drew an image of you
and I suffered:

I couldn't take the moon-shaped puddle
so that I could have – at least –
your image reflected in the water.

Mist in the afternoon

Let me weep now,
because soon I won't have the time.

Let me love you now,
because tomorrow
life will weigh more heavily on me.

Don't tell me that this dream
will end.

Don't tell me that hope
disappears like mist in the afternoon.

I don't want to know that I am lying to myself
and that this pain which little by little
is taking over the space in my heart
is the only truth.

THE MORN'S MORN

Xaqje'are

Kinwil ri numam
kuchararej kajwinaq lajuj ujunab'
xaq ruk'ri uchaket
ri kub'an kawinaq lajuj junab'.

Xek'iy ri tzoloj che'
par ri ub'oq'och
su xekanajkan chila'.

Himself

I see my grandfather
dragging his ninety years
with the same jacket
as he wore at fifty.

Willows have etched their roots
in his eyes
forever.

Himsel

I see ma granfaither
harlin his ninety years
wi the same jaiket
he had on at fifty.

Sauchs hae scartit their ruits
in his een
for aye.

The deid-kist

The deid-kist wis
the colour o a tree.

They pit it in the kirkyaird
aside the silence
o the ithers.

When they cam back hame
she felt as if
the wecht o a stane
had been taen aff her.

'He's awa…he's awa,'
she tellt her bairns.

That husband battered her.

That is ma mither.
Yon wis ma faither.

Freedom

Blackies, gleds and doos
land on kirks and courthooses
jist as they dae on rocks,
trees and fences…

and they keech on them
wi aw the freedom o yin that kens
that god and justice
belang the sowl.

Prayer

In the kirks
ye canna hear ocht
but the prayer
o the trees
turnt intae pews.

Nicanor

He wid staun for oors on a street corner
whustlin,
laughin intae himsel,
or chuckin stanes.

'How come ye got oot
the bamhoose, Nica?'

'Cos the bams
were daein ma fuckin heid in.'

The morn's morn, mibbe

Maister Ajiatas,
mair boolie-backit day by day,
warkin the land o ither folk.

In his hert
hope isna smoored,
'wene chweq ku k' ex uwech wa' '.

(the morn's morn mibbe, this will aw chynge)

Auld claes

Ma auld claes
Are faur-through wi wark.

When I gaed oot intae the street
I left the holes ben the hoose
and I gaed oot wi the clouts on ma sowl,
ma son's smile,
and ma lassie's look.

Yin o thae

The puir, we dinna hae nae freens,
jist chiels that chum us alang the road.

I steekit ma auld shoon
and I gaed wi fient a bawbee
in ma pooches.

I kent the herbs
that turn tae hinny
on the slaiverless tung.

I am yin o thae that traivel
and ilka time
are left mair ahint by dreams.

In spite o awthin
I am yin o thae that disna bury
hope.

That efternune

Ae efternune he cawed me:
his een were bigger,
his gaze seemed tae gaither
aw that he wantit tae tak.

His wabster's vyce,
cadger o dools,
crabbit and sad:
awready it wis a faurawa vyce.

He'd been doun the road a bittock.
Me, I wis jist settin oot.

I ran ahint his fitsteps
wi a wee pooch
the size o ma strenth.

And that efternune,
och, that efternune!

On the road tae the kirkyaird
I grat.

I cam back alane
and became a man.

Pak'lom mountain

How beautiful was the mountainside
full of old cypresses.

If you could have seen
how pretty the mountain was
full of ghosts
amongst the palisades,

until a stupid mayor
ordered all the trees cut down.

Since then
the mountainside looks so sad.

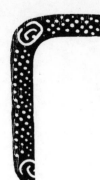

Yellow flower of
the graveyards

Coyotes howl and break the night silence:
they play with the wind.
'It's a bad sign…'

Before, the owls hooted from time to time,
now they hoot more often.
'It doesn't augur well.'

A wind of death blows down the peak,
icy, it bites like a dog with rabies…
and the flowers curl up, they're frightened
and before midday, they wither away.

If only we could go back to those times
when the earth sang with men.

Today the shoots are cut off before time,
the cries of the children go unheeded, nobody cares:
the sky opens its mouth and swallows
the cry which smothers death.

Why are we Indians persecuted?
What have we done to you, Guatemala?
Why is there this hatred, this thirst for blood?

We owe nothing to death.

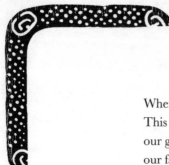

Where can we run, why flee?
This is where our ancestors made their homes,
our grandfathers were born here,
our fathers were born here,
we were born here,
here our children will be born;
this is our land.
Why should we seek refuge anywhere else?
Why should we become pilgrims?

Little birds of the mountainsides:
Güis-güil, Tuc-tuc, Chaper-pantuj,
come and cry with me,
I am so very sad and
the wound hurts.
Our bundle is full of suffering,
we hide so that no one can mock our suffering,
we drown our tears in the streams.

Maybe it's a crime to be an Indian?
For five hundred years
we've been persecuted.
They kill Indians for whatever reason:
they've razed whole towns and villages…

Lord of the heavens,
Lord of the earth:
where were you when these things happened?

Why did you agree to these massacres?

We are poor, but hard workers.
Our crime is to be honourable.

We live in poverty and sadness
and even so, we resist from the
depths of our culture.

Where did this curse come from?
From whence came this whirlwind
with the jaws of a huge animal,
with eyes that seem deeper than the depths of the ravine,
which snuffs out lives
to preserve the darkness of terror?

The animals of the mountainside
fight amongst themselves
but they don't kill each other.

Erupt, volcanoes!
Burn, fires!
Tremble, earth, split open
and swallow everything, everything, everything!

No one wants peace here,
here there is a hunger for death,

men are blind,
the laws are deaf,
the paths are crooked...
The night shows no sign of ending,
death stalks drunkenly,
replete with blood,
the shadows of murder
spread their wings and shut out the light,
bats dance in the flames of hate:
black fire!

Jawchi coj be wi? chi xe coj'iwi ri q'a mam,

chi xe co'jiwi ri q'a tat,

chi xoj alaxicwi...

Justice doesn't speak our language,
justice doesn't reach down to the poor people,
justice doesn't use rope sandals,
justice doesn't walk barefoot
on earthen paths...

Screams here,
screams there,
screams on every side.
Power has its way, it makes your hair stand on end;

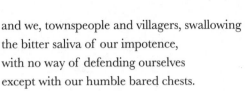
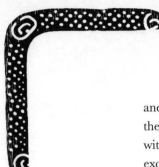

and we, townspeople and villagers, swallowing
the bitter saliva of our impotence,
with no way of defending ourselves
except with our humble bared chests.

We walk the streets, the paths,
the passageways, with fear:
who's walking behind us?
Who's walking in front?
What was that noise?
Every shadow makes us jump,
the screech of a vulture startles us,
even a leaf falling from a tree
makes our souls tremble.

The doors of evil have been opened
and death's messengers
carry out their slaughter by day and night ...

The slopes are full of Coxguaj:
'the yellow flower of the graveyards',
and the yellow afternoon,
the same yellow as the flower of death,
dies behind the hillside.

Sun!
Turn to smoke, stain the sky,
burn the earth. We are in mourning,

my people,
my blood,
my kin.

The grey horizon is sad.
Here, they have forgotten shame,
fires burn in the roadways,
poverty, hunger and loneliness
drag themselves through the dust.
Little children chew on misery,
they swallow fright and run without knowing where.
How sad it is to be an orphan!

In this country of illiterates
you cannot call us atheists:
but then, in which god do they believe,
those with no respect for human life?

We are many,
you cannot deny our presence,
silent but not dumb:
our native flutes,
our drums,
our little rural marimbas,
the cofradias*, the masked dances,
the feast days of our villages –
aren't they the voice of our people?

* In each cofradia a married couple takes charge of a saint's image during the year, their charge culminating in a three-day-long celebration of the saint's day. There are seven levels of responsibility. Before the Conquest this system was used to train men to worship the gods and keep the peace in their communities, attainment of the highest level being a requirement for eligibility to hold the office of local 'mayor'.

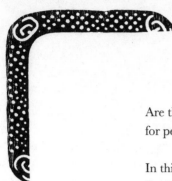

Are they not evidence of our desire
for peace and tranquillity?

In this country, they only regard us
for their own selfish ends:
politicians stamp on us,
landowners exploit us,
religions confuse us,
and the tourist offices exhibit us…

All this breaks my heart.
Brother,
shall we drink a glass of clear water,
shall we sing the blackbird's song together?
Let us embrace and forget our troubles.
I can hardly see you amidst my tears.
Seek your happiness today
because tomorrow – who knows?

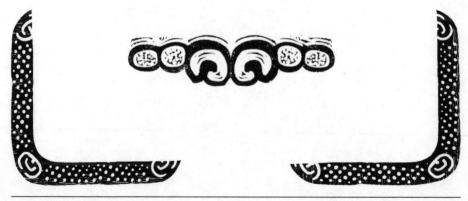

A note on the K'iche'
language and pronunciation

K'iche' is a Mayan language spoken by about one million people in the central highlands of Guatemala. The K'iche' language has played a central role in the Mayan cultural revitalisation movement and has a long literary tradition including such works as the **Popol Wuuj** (**Popol Vuh**), the Mayan creation story, and **Rabinal Achi,** a dance drama which tells of the victory of the Achi' people over the K'iche' prince.

a	as in the *a* of 'father'
ä	as in the *o* of 'mother'
b'	as in *b* but pronounced with the throat closed to form a glottal stop
ch	as in the *ch* of 'child'
ch'	pronounced as for *ch* but with the throat closed to provide a glottalised *ch*
e	as in the *e* of 'lent'
gu	as in the *wh* of 'whisky'
i	as in the *ee* of 'feel'
j	as in the *ch* of 'loch'
k	as in the *k* of 'king'
k'	pronounced with the tongue in the same position as in the *k* but with the throat closed to provide a glottalised *k*
l	pronounced like the English *l*, but with the tongue moved forward to contact the upper incisor teeth
m	as in the *m* of 'mat'
n	as in the *n* of 'nut'
o	as in the *o* of 'own'
p	a shortened version of the English *p*
q	pronounced further back in the throat than the English *k*, like the Kh in 'Khartoum'
q'	pronounced with the tongue in the same position as the Kich'e *q*, but with the throat closed to produce a glottal sound
r	similar to the Spanish *r*, pronounced with a brief tap of the tongue against the roof of the mouth
s	as the *s* in 'sit'
t	similar to the English *t* but shorter
t'	similar to the above, but with the throat closed to produce a glottal sound
tz	as in the *ts* sound in 'cats'
tz'	similar to the above, but with the throat closed to produce a glottal sound
x	as in the *sh* of 'shut'

The stress, unless noted, is usually on the final syllable of the word.

The Maya civilisation used a vigesimal (twenty-based) numeric system, with each number represented by a combination of three symbols: zero (a shell shape), one (a dot) and five(a bar). In our decimal system, a one (1) followed by a zero (0) represents ten. In the Mayan system, a one (dot) followed by a zero (shell shape) represents twenty.